COLUMBIA SLAVIC STUDIES, a series of the
DEPARTMENT OF SLAVIC LANGUAGES, COLUMBIA UNIVERSITY
ERNEST J. SIMMONS, General Editor

BIBLIOGRAPHY OF

SLAVIC PHILOLOGY

Edited by William E. Harkins

KING'S CROWN PRESS

Columbia University   1951   New York

Published in Great Britain, Canada, and India
by Geoffrey Cumberlege, Oxford University Press, London,
Toronto, and Bombay

MANUFACTURED IN THE UNITED STATES OF AMERICA

ACKNOWLEDGMENT

The preparation and publication of the several
series of works under SLAVIC STUDIES have been made
possible by a grant from the Rockefeller Foundation to
the Department of Slavic Languages of Columbia University.

Ernest J. Simmons
Executive Officer

EDITOR'S PREFACE

This booklet represents a unique attempt at a brief but comprehensive bibliography of the most important works, in both Slavic and non-Slavic languages, in the field of Slavic philology. It is an outgrowth of an older mimeographed bibliography prepared by Professor Roman Jakobson for student use, when he was a member of the staff of the Department of Slavic Languages at Columbia University, and later revised by him at Harvard University. The entire work has subsequently been reviewed by members of the staff of the Department, including Professors Ad. Stender-Petersen, Manfred Kridl, Karl H. Menges, and Dr. Gojko Ružičić. A number of additions and modifications were made in the original bibliography, and in this revised and printed form it is hoped that the compilation will be of wider service to teachers in the field, as well as students, and to librarians.

The bibliography seeks to include the most important works, without reference to their availability in certain libraries. This has been done in order that it might serve as a guide to American libraries and to scholars acquiring collections in the fields of Slavic philology, rather than reflect the biases or omissions of any particular collection.

The subject matter of philology is here conceived as comprising both linguistic science, synchronic and diachronic (practical textbooks and dictionaries have likewise been included as student aids), as well as prehistory and early cultural history of the Slavic peoples. Literature and history have been excluded as too extensive subjects for treatment on an all-Slavic level. The Department plans a series of bibliographies for the separate Slavic cultures and literatures, of which a Czechoslovak Bibliography is already in print. Folk literature has likewise been excluded, but has been treated in the Department's *Bibliography of Slavic Folk Literature*, which will appear very shortly.

Acknowledgment is made to Drs. Gojko Ružičić and Ludwik Krzyżanowski, and to Mr. John Washburn, for their help in verifying certain bibliographical data, and to Mr. Walter Roziewski for his painstaking work in vari-typing the text in the original languages and alphabets. Since some of the works themselves were unavailable for checking, verification of bibliographical information has been impossible, and some errors or omissions have doubt-less occured.

W. E. Harkins

C O N T E N T S

CONTENTS

BIBLIOGRAPHY OF

SLAVIC PHILOLOGY

PHILOLOGY AND GENERAL LINGUISTICS

Foundations of Linguistics

1. Sapir, Edward. Language. New York, 1921 and 1939.

2. -----. "Communication," "Dialect," "Language,"
   "Symbolism," Encyclopedia of the Social
   Sciences, Vols. IV, V, IX, XIV, 1931-34.

3. Bloomfield, Leonard. Language. New York, 1933, 1938,
   and 1948.

4. Saussure, Ferdinand de. Cours de linguistique
   générale. Lausanne, 1916; Paris, 1922 and 1931.
   Russian translation, Moscow, 1933.

5. Kořínek, J.M. Úvod do jazykozpytu. Bratislava, 1948.

6. Nida, Eugene A. Morphology: the descriptive analysis
   of words. Ann Arbor, 1949.

7. Jespersen, Otto. The Philosophy of Grammar. New York
   and London, 1924 and later editions.

Phonology

8. Sweet, Henry A. Primer of Phonetics (3rd. edition).
   Oxford, 1906.

9. Поливанов, Е. Д. Введение в языкознание. Leningrad,
   1928.

10. Martinet, André. Phonology as Functional Phonetics.
    London, 1949.

3

11. Troubetzkoy, N.S. Principes de Phonologie. Paris,
    1949. German edition as: Grundzüge der
    Phonologie. (Travaux du Cercle linguistique
    de Prague, No. 7.) Prague, 1939.

12. Pike, K.L. Phonemics: a technique for reducing
    languages to writing. (University of
    Michigan publications, Linguistics, No. 3)
    Ann Arbor, 1947.

13. Jakobson, Roman. "Observations sur le classement
    phonologique des consonnes," Proceedings of
    the Third International Congress of Phonetic
    Sciences. (Ghent, 1938), pp. 34-41.

14. -----. "On the Identification of Phonemic Entities,"
    Travaux du Cercle linguistique de Copenhague,
    V (1949).

Literary Theory

15. Wellek, René and Austin Warren. Theory of Litera-
    ture. New York, 1949.

16. Томашевский, Б.В. Теория литературы. Leningrad,
    1931.

17. -----. Писатель и книга. Leningrad, 1928.

18. Lotz, John. "Notes on Structural Analysis in
    Metrics," Helicon: Revue internationale
    des problèmes généraux de la littérature
    (Amsterdam), IV (1942).

19. Jakobson, Roman. "Metrika," Ottův slovník naučný
    nové doby, Dodatky, IV, 1 (1935), 213-218.

Essentials of Comparative Philology

20. Meillet, Antoine. Introduction à l'étude comparative des langues indoeuropéennes (7th edition). Paris, 1934.

21. ----. La méthode comparative en linguistique historique. Oslo, 1925.

22. Deeters, Gerhard. "Vergleichende Sprachforschung," Lehrbuch der Völkerkunde. Edited by K.T. Preuss. Stuttgart, 1939, pp. 211-236.

History of Linguistics

23. Pedersen, Holger. Linguistic Science in the Nineteenth Century. Translated by J.W. Spargo. Cambridge, Mass., 1931.

24. Milewski, Tadeusz. Zarys językoznawstwa ogólnego, Vol. I (Prace etnologiczne, Vol. I.) Lublin and Cracow, 1947.

Survey of the Languages of the World

25. Meillet, Antoine and Marcel Cohen, eds. Les langues du monde. Paris, 1924.

26. Schmidt, Wilhelm. Die Sprachfamilien und Sprachenkreise der Erde. Heidelberg, 1926.

27. Milewski, Tadeusz. Zarys językoznawstwa ogólnego, Vol. II. (Prace etnologiczne, Vol. II.) Lublin and Cracow, 1947.

Dictionaries

28. Walde, Alois. Vergleichendes Wörterbuch der indogermanischen Sprachen. 3 vols. Edited by Julius Pokorny. Berlin, 1927-1932.

29. Pokorny, Julius. Indogermanisches etymologisches Wörterbuch. 3 vols. Bern, 1948-1949.

Dictionaries of Linguistic Terminology

30. Marouzeau, Jules. Lexique de la terminologie linguistique. Paris, 1943.

31. Жирков,Л. И. Лингвистический словарь. Moscow, 1946.

32. Дурново, Николай. Грамматический словарь. Moscow, 1924.

COMPARATIVE SLAVIC PHILOLOGY

Comparative Linguistics

33. Jakobson, Roman. Slavic Languages. New York, 1949.

34. Trautmann, Reinhold. Die slavischen Völker und Sprachen. Göttingen, 1947.

35. Nahtigal, Rajko. Slovanski jeziki. Vol. I. Ljubljana, 1938.

36. Broch, Olaf. Slavische Phonetik. Heidelberg, 1911. Russian version as: Очерк физиологии славянской речи. St. Petersburg, 1910.

37. Meillet, Antoine. Le slave commun. Paris, 1924.

38. Mikkola, J. J. Urslavische Grammatik. 3 vols. Heidelberg, 1913-1950.

39. Wijk, Nicolaas van. "Les Langues slaves," Le Monde slave, III (July-Sept. 1937), IV (Oct. 1937) 14-40, 369-395.

40. Vondrák, Wenzel. Vergleichende slavische Grammatik. 2 vols. Göttingen, 1924-1928.

41. Hujer, Oldřich. Slovanská deklinace jmenná. Prague, 1910.

42. Stang, C.S.   Das slavische und baltische Verbum. Oslo, 1942.

43. Regnell, C.G.   Über den Ursprung des slavischen Verbalaspektes. Lund, 1944.

44. Miklosich, Franz.   Vergleichende Grammatik der slavischen Sprachen. Vol. III, Syntax. Vienna, 1876.

45. Jakobson, Roman.   Remarques sur l'évolution phonologique du russe comparée à celle des autres langues slaves.   (Travaux du Cercle linguistique de Prague, No. 2.) Prague, 1929, pp. 1-118.

46. Kuryłowicz, Jerzy.   "Intonation et morphologie en slave commun," Rocznik Slawistyczny (Cracow), XIV (1938), 1-66.

47. Bubrich, D.V.   "Du Systeme d'accentuation en slave commun," Revue des études slaves (Paris), VI (1926), 175-215.

48. Senn, Alfred.   "On the Degree of Kinship between Slavic and Baltic," Slavonic and East European Review (London), XX (1941), 251-265.

49. Szemerényi, O.   "Sur l'unité linguistique balto-slave," Etudes slaves et roumaines (Budapest), I, fascicules 2-3 (1948), 65-85, 159-173.

50. Rozwadowski, Jan.   "Stosunki leksykalne mędzy językami słowiańskiemi a irańskiemi," Rocznik oryentalistyczny (Cracow), I (1914-15), 95-110.

51. Meillet, Antoine.   "Le vocabulaire slave et le vocabulaire indo-iranien," Revue des études slaves (Paris), VI (1926), 165-174.

52. Stender-Petersen, Ad.   Slavisch-germanische Lehnwortkunde. Göteborg, 1927.

53. Kiparsky, Valentin.   Die gemeinslavischen Lehnwörter aus dem germanischen. Helsinki, 1934.

54. Miklosich, Franz. Die Bildung der slavischen
        Personen- und Ortsnamen. Heidelberg, 1927

55. Lehr-Spławiński, Tadeusz. Zarys dziejów języków
        literackich słowiańskich (Biblioteka
        slawistyczna, Vol. IX.) Lwow, 1929.

56. Дурново, Николай. "Мысли и предположения о
        происхождении старославянского языка и
        славянских алфавитов," Byzantinoslavica
        (Prague), I (1929), 48-85.

57. ------. "Еще о происхождении старославянского языка
        и письма," Byzantinoslavica (Prague), III
        (1931), 68-78.

History of Slavic Philology

58. Nahtigal, Rajko. Uvod v slovansko filologijo.
        Ljubljana, 1949.

59. Ягич, И.В. История славянской филологии.
        St. Petersburg, 1910.

Cultural Prehistory and History

of the Slavic Peoples

60. Cross, S.H. Slavic Civilization through the Ages.
        Cambridge, Mass., 1948.

61. Niederle, Lubor. Slovanské starožitnosti. 2 vols.
        Prague, 1902-1934. French version as:
        Manuel de l'antiquité slave. 2 vols.
        Paris 1923-1926. Russian version as: Быт
        и культура древних славян. Prague, 1924.

62. Lehr-Spławiński, Tadeusz. O pochodzeniu i
        praojczyźnie Słowian. Poznan, 1946.

63. Vasmer, Max. Die alten Bevölkerungsverhältnisse
        Russlands im Lichte der Sprachforschung.
        Berlin, 1941.

64. -----. Untersuchungen über die ältesten Wohnsitze
der Slaven: Die Iranier in Südrussland.
Leipzig, 1923.

65. -----. Beiträge zur historischen Völkerkunde
Osteuropas. (Sitzungsberichte der
preussischen Akademie der Wissenschaften,
Vols. XVI, XVIII, XIX.) Berlin, 1932-1936.

66. Czekanowski, Jan. Wstęp do historji Słowian. Lwow,
1927.

67. Kostrzewski, Józef. Zarys dziejów i kultury
Prasłowian. Poznan, 1946.

68. Weingart, Miloš. Slovanská vzájemnost. Bratislava,
1926.

69. Strakhovsky, L.I., ed. A Handbook of Slavic Studies.
Cambridge, Mass., 1949.

70. Mousset, Albert. Le monde slave (2nd. edition).
Paris, 1946.

Dictionaries

71. Miklosich, Franz. Dictionnaire abrégé de six
langues slaves (russe, vieux-slave, bulgaire,
serbe, tchèque et polonaise) ainsi que
français et allemand. St. Petersburg and
Moscow, 1885.

72. Berneker, Erich. Slavisches etymologisches
Wörterbuch, Vol. I. Heidelberg, 1913.

73. Trautmann, Reinhold. Baltisch-Slawisches Wörterbuch.
Göttingen, 1923.

OLD CHURCH SLAVONIC

Grammar and Phonology

74. Diels, Paul. Altkirchenslavische Grammatik. 2 vols.
    Heidelberg, 1932-1934.

75. Kul'bakin, S.M. Le vieux slave. 2 vols. Paris,
    1929.

76. Leskien, August. Handbuch der altbulgarischen
    (altkirchenslavischen) Sprache. Heidelberg,
    1922. Photo-lithoprint reproduction,
    Ann Arbor, 1945.

77. -----. Grammatik der altbulgarischen (altkirchen-
    slavischen) Sprache. Heidelberg, 1909.

78. Trubetzkoy, N.S. Altkirchenslavische Sprache.
    Vienna, 1933.

79. Wijk, Nicolaas van. Geschichte der altkirchen-
    slavischen Sprache, Vol. I. Berlin, 1931.

80. Vaillant, André. Manuel du vieux slave. 2 vols.
    Paris, 1948.

81. Meillet, Antoine. Etudes sur l'étymologie et le
    vocabulaire du vieux slave. 2 vols.
    Paris, 1902-1905.

82. Трубецкой, Н.С. "Общеславянский элемент в русской
    культуре," К проблеме русского самопо-
    знания. Paris, 1927. English translation
    as: The Common Slavic Element in Russian
    Culture. Edited by Leon Stilman. New
    York, 1949.

83. Weingart, Miloš. Československý typ cirkevnej
    slovančiny. Bratislava, 1949.

Paleography

84. Vajs, Josef. Rukovět hlaholské paleografie. Prague, 1932.

85. Карский, Е.Ф. Славянская кирилловская палеография. Leningrad, 1928.

Texts

86. Vondrák, Wenzel. Kirchenslavische Chrestomathie. Göttingen, 1910. Czech version: Brno, 1925.

87. Каринский, Н.М. Хрестоматия по древне-церковно-славянскому и русскому языкам, Vol. I. St. Petersburg, 1911.

88. Weingart, Miloš. Teksty ke studiu jazyka a písemnictví staroslověnského. Prague, 1938.

89. Berneker, Erich. Slavische Chrestomathie. Strassburg, 1902.

Dictionaries

90. Miklosich, Franz. Lexicon palaeoslovenico-graeco-latinum. Vienna, 1862-1865.

91. Słoński, Stanisław. Index verborum de Euchologium Sinaiticum. Warsaw, 1934.

92. Meyer, K.H. Altkirchenslavisch-griechisches Wörterbuch des Codex Suprasliensis. Glückstadt-Hamburg, 1935.

Dictionaries in Editions

of Old Church Slavonic Texts

93. Jagić, Vatroslav. Quattuor evangeliorum codex
Marianus glagoliticus. Berlin, 1883.

94. Vondrák, Václav. Glagolitica Clozûv. Prague, 1893.

95. Северьянов, Сергей. Синаиская псалтырь. Petrograd,
1922.

96. Щепкич, В.Н. Саввина книга. St. Petersburg, 1903.

Church Slavonic Culture

97. Jakobson, Roman. "The Beginnings of National Self-
Determination in Europe," The Review of
Politics, VII, 1 (1945), 29-42.

98. Cross, S.H. "The Results of the Conversion of the
Slavs from Byzantium," Annuaire de
l'Institut de philologie et d'histoire
orientales et slaves, Université de
Bruxelles, VII (1939-44), 71-82.

99. Dvornik, František. Les Slaves, Byzance et Rome
au IXe siècle. Paris, 1926.

100. -----. Les légendes de Constantin et de Méthode
vues de Byzance. Prague, 1933.

101. -----. The Making of Central and Eastern Europe.
London, 1949.

EAST SLAVIC LANGUAGES

Introduction to East Slavic Languages

102. Дурново, Николай. Введение в историю русского
языка, Vol. I. Brno, 1927.

103. Третьяков, П.Н. Восточнославянские племена. Moscow, 1948.

104. Шахматов, А.А. Введение в курс истории русского языка, Vol. I. Petrograd, 1916 and Moscow, 1938.

Russian

Modern Russian

105. Булаховский, Л.А. Курс русского литературного языка. Kharkov, 1937.

106. Шахматов, А.А. Очерк современного русского литературного языка (4th edition). Moscow, 1941.

107. Авакумов, С. Современный русский литературчый язык. Moscow, 1942.

108. Аванесов, Р.И. and В.Н. Сидоров. Очерк грамматики русского литературного языка, Vol. I. Moscow, 1945.

109. Виноградов, В.В. Русскии язык. Moscow, 1947.

110. Обнорский, С.П. Именное склонение в современном русском языке. 2 Vols. Leningrad, 1927-1931.

111. Jakobson, Roman. "Beitrag zur allgemeinen Kasuslehre; Gesamtbedeutungen der russischen Kasus," Travaux du Cercle linguistique de Prague, VI (1936), 240-288.

112. ------. "Russian Conjugation," Word, IV (1948), 155-167.

113. ------. "Zur Struktur des russischen Verbums," Charisteria Gvilelmo Mathesio oblata. Prague, 1932, pp. 74-84.

13

114. Karcevski, Serge. Système du verbe russe. Prague, 1927.

115. Шахматов,А.А. Синтаксис русского языка (2nd. edition). Leningrad, 1941.

116. Пешковский, А.Р. Русский синтаксис в научном освещении (2nd. edition). Moscow, 1920.

117. Boyanus, S.C. A Manual of Russian Pronunciation. London, 1935.

118. Trubetzkoy, N.S. Das morphonologische System der russischen Sprache. (Travaux du Cercle linguistique de Prague, V, 2). Prague, 1934.

119. Богородицкий, В.А. Фонетика русского. языка в свете экспериментальных данных. Kazan, 1930.

History and Dialectology of Russian

120. Дурново, Николай. Очерк истории русского языка. Moscow, 1924.

121. Винокур, Г.О. Русский язык. Moscow, 1945. French version as: La langue russe. Paris, 1947.

122. Якубинский, Л. Очерки по истории древнерусского языка. Moscow, 1945.

123. Шахматов, А.А. Курс истории русского языка, Vol. III (Учение о формах). St. Petersburg, 1911.

124. ------. Очерк древнейшего периода истории русского языка. Petrograd, 1915.

125. Unbegaun, Boris. La langue russe au XVIe siècle (1500-1555). Paris, 1935.

126. Истрина, Е.С. "Синтаксические явления синодального списка I Новгородской летописи," Известия Отделения русского языка и словесности Российской Академии наук, XXIV, 2 (1919), 1-172, XXVI (1921), 207-239.

127. Дементьев, А. Сборник задач и упражнений по
     исторической грамматике русского языка.
     Moscow, 1946.

128. Дурново, Николай. Хрестоматия по истории русского
     языка. Moscow, 1914.

129. Обнорский, С.П. and С.Г. Бархударов. Хрестоматия
     по истории русского языка. 2 vols.
     Leningrad, 1938-1948.

130. Аванесов, Р.И. Очерки русской диалектологии.
     Moscow, 1949.

131. Еремин, С.А. and И.А. Фалев. Русская диалектология.
     Moscow, 1928.

132. Дурново, Николай and Д.Н. Ушаков. Хрестоматия по
     великорусской диалектологии. Moscow,
     1910.

133. Селищев, А.М. Диалектологический очерк Сибири.
     Irkutsk, 1921.

Development of Standard Russian

134. Булаховский, Л.А. Исторический комментарий к
     литературному русскому языку. Kharkov,
     1937.

135. Виноградов, В.В. Очерки по истории русского
     литературного языка XVII-XIX вв. Moscow,
     1934.

136. Булаховский, Л.А. Русский литературный язык первой
     половины XIX века. Kharkov-Kiev, 1941.

137. Jakobson, Roman. "Slavische Sprachfragen in der
     Sovjetunion," Slavische Rundschau (Prague),
     V (1934), 324-343.

Paleography

138. Щепкин, В.Н. Учебник русской палеографии. Moscow, 1918.

139. Чаев, Н.С. Русская палеография. Moscow, 1946.

History of Russian Philological Science

140. Обнорский, С.П. and В.В. Виноградов. Русская наука о русском языке. (Московский университет, Ученые записки, Vol CVI.) Moscow, 1946.

141. Murra, John V., Robert M. Hankin and Fred Holling, eds. The Soviet Linguistic Controversy. New York, 1951.

Dictionaries

142. Ушаков, Д.С. Толковый словарь русского языка. 4 vols. Moscow, 1935-1940 and 1948. Photo-lithoprint reproduction, Ann Arbor, 1948.

143. Ожегов, С.И. and С.П. Обнорский. Словарь русского языка. Moscow, 1949.

144. Даль, Владимир. Толковый словарь живого велико-русского языка. 4 vols. 3rd. edition. St. Petersburg, 1903-1909. Reprint, revised by Jan Baudouin de Courtenay. Tokyo, 1934.

145. Срезневский, И.И. Материалы для словаря древне-русского языка по письменным памятникам. 3 vols. St. Petersburg, 1890-1912.

146. Кочин, Г.Е. Материалы для терминологического словаря древней России. Moscow, 1937.

147. Ларин, Б.А. Проект древне-русского словаря. Leningrad, 1936.

148. Преображенский, А.В. Этимологический словарь русского языка. 3 vols. Moscow, 1910-1949. Photo-lithoprint edition to be prepared at Columbia University.

149. Смирницкий, А.И. Русско-английский словарь. Moscow, 1949.

150. Müller, V.K. Russian-English Dictionary. New York, 1944.

151. ------. English-Russian Dictionary. New York and Philadelphia, 1944.

152. Александров, А. (pseudonym). Полный англо-русский словарь. New York, 1909.

Ukrainian

Modern Ukrainian

153. Luckyj, George and Jaroslav Rudnickyj. A Modern Ukrainian Grammar. Minneapolis, 1949.

154. Кульбакин, С.М. Украинский язык. Kharkov, 1919.

155. Булаховский, Л.А. Загальний курс української мови. Kharkov, n.d.

156. Сімович, Василь. Граматика української мови. Kiev, 1919.

157. Синявський, О. Норми української літературної мови. Kiev, 1931.

158. Курило, О. Уваги до сучасної української літературної мови. Cracow-Lwow, 1942.

159. Смеречинський, С. Нариси з української синтакси. Kiev, 1932.

160. Ziłyński, Jan. Opis fonetyczny języka
ukraińskiego. (Polska akademja\umiejęt-
ności, Prace Komisji językowej, No. 19).
Cracow, 1932.

History and Dialectology of Ukrainian

161. Шахматов, А.А. and Агат Кримський. Нариси з исторії
української мови та хрестоматія. Kiev,
1924. Russian version in: Украинский
народ в его прошлом и настоящем, Vol. I.
Petrograd, 1915.

162. Грунський, М. and П. Ковалев. Нариси з исторії
української мови. Lwow, 1941.

163. Тимченко, Євген. Курс исторії українського язика.
Kiev, 1927.

164. Житецкий, П.И. Очерк литературной истории мало-
русского наречия в XVII и XVIII вв. Kiev,
1889.

165. Ганцов, В. Діялектологічна класифікація
українських говорів. Kiev, 1923.

166. Жілинський, Іван. Карта українських говорів.
Warsaw, 1933.

167. Панькевич, Іван. /Українські говори Підкарпатської
Руси і сумежних областей. Prague, 1938.

168. Дурново, Николай. Хрестоматия по малорусской
диалектологии. Moscow, 1910.

Dictionaries

169. Грінченко, В. Словарь української мови. 4 vols.
Kiev, 1907-1909, and Berlin, 1924.

170. Тимченко, Євген. Историчний словник українського
язика, Vol. I. Kharkov, 1930.

171. Kuzel'a, Zenon and J.B. Rudnyc'kyj. Ukrainisch-
     deutsches Wörterbuch. Leipzig, 1943.

172. Калинович, М.Я. Русско-украинский словарь. Moscow,
     1948.

Bjelo-Russian

Modern Bjelo-Russian

173. Карзон, А. and М. Жыркевіч. Граматіка беларускай
     мовы. 2 vols. Minsk, 1946.

174. Беларуская Акадэмія навук. Беларуская граматіка.
     2 vols. Minsk, 1936-1939.

175. Ломтев, Т. Беларуская граматіка, фанэтіка і правопіс.
     Minsk, 1936.

176. Станкевич, Я. Падручнік крывіцкае (беларускае)
     мовы. Regensburg, 1947.

History and Dialectology

of Bjelo-Russian

177. Расторгуев, П.А. "Белорусская речь в ее современном
     и прошлом состоянии", Курс белорусоведения.
     Moscow, 1920.

178. Карский, Е.Ф. Белорусы. 2 vols. Warsaw, 1903-1912.

179. Stang, C.S. Die westrussische Kanzleisprache des
     Grossfürstentums Litauen. Oslo, 1935.

180. Бузж, П.А. Спроба лінгвыстічноі гэографіі Беларусі.
     Minsk, 1928.

181. Расторгуев, П.А. Северско-белорусский говор.
     Leningrad, 1927.

182. Stankević, J. "Stan badań nad klasyfikacją
        dialektów języka białoruskiego,"
        Balticoslavica (Vilna), II (1936), 108-
        128.

        Dictionaries

183. Чосович, И.И. Словарь белорусского наречия.
        St. Petersburg, 1870.

184. Байков, М. and С. Чекрашэвіч. Беларуска-расійскі
        словнік. Minsk, 1925.

185. Колас, Якуб (pseudonym of К. Міцкевич). Русско-
        белорусский словарь. Minsk, 1946.

WESTERN SLAVIC LANGUAGES

Introduction to Western Slavic Languages

186. Селищев, А.М. Славянское языкознание, Vol. I
        (Западно-славянские языки). Moscow,
        1941.

187. Niederle, Lubor. Slovanské starožitnosti, Vol. I,
        Part III (Původ a počátky Slovanů
        západních). Prague, 1913.

Polish

Modern Polish

188. Grappin, Henri. Grammaire de la langue polonaise.
        Paris, 1942.

189. Gaertner, Henryk. Gramatyka współczesnego języka polskiego. 3 vols. Lwow, 1931-1934.

190. Szober, Stanisław. Gramatyka języka polskiego (revised edition). Lwow, 1923.

191. Klemensiewicz, Zenon. Składania opisowa współczesnej polszczyzny kulturalnej. Cracow, 1937.

192. Rozwadowski, Jan and Kazimierz Nitsch. Głosowania języka polskiego. Cracow, 1925.

193. Grappin, Henri. Introduction phonétique à l'étude de la langue polonaise. Paris; 1944.

History and Dialectology of Polish

194. Benni, Tytus, Jan Łoś, Kazimierz Nitsch and Henryk Ułaszyn. Gramatyka języka polskiego. Cracow, 1923.

195. Lehr-Spławiński,Tadeusz. Język polski, pochodzenie, powstanie, rozwój. Warsaw, 1947.

196. Brückner, Aleksander. Dzieje języka polskiego (3rd. edition). Warsaw, 1925.

197. Słoński, Stanisław. Historja języka polskiego w zarysie. Lwow-Warsaw, 1934.

198. Łoś, Jan. Krótka gramatyka historyczna języka polskiego. Warsaw, 1927.

199. ------. Gramatyka polska. 2 vols. Lwow, 1922-1927.

200. Nieminen, Eino. "Beiträge zur altpolnischen Syntax," Annales Academiae Scientiarum Fennicae (Helsinki), XLIII, 3 (1939-1940).

201. Łoś, Jan. Pisownia polska w przeszłości i obecnie. Cracow, 1917.

202. Vrtel-Wierczyński, Stefan. Wybór tekstów staro-
     polskich. Lwow, 1930.

203. Taszycki, Witold. Najdawniejsze zabytki języka
     polskiego. Cracow, 1927.

204. Nitsch, Kazimierz. Wybór polskich tekstów
     gwarowych. Lwow, 1929.

Dictionaries

205. Kryński, Adam, J.A. Karłowicz and Władysław
     Niedźwiedzki. Słownik języka polskiego.
     8 vols. Warsaw, 1900-1927.

206. Karłowicz, J.A. Słownik gwar polskich. 6 vols.
     Cracow, 1900-1911.

207. Krasnowolski, Antoni and Władysław Niedźwiedzki.
     Słownik staropolski. 2 vols. Warsaw, 1914.

208. Brückner, Aleksander. Słownik etymologiczny języka
     polskiego. 2 vols. Cracow, 1927.

209. Chodzko, Aleksander. Dokładny słownik polsko-
     angielski i angielsko-polski. Chicago,
     n.d.

Kashubian and Polabian

210. Lorentz, Friedrich. Gramatyka pomorska. 7 parts.
     Poznan, 1927-1936.

211. ——. Geschichte der pomoranischen (kaschubischen)
     Sprache. Berlin, 1925.

212. ——, Adam Fischer and Tadeusz Lehr-Spławiński.
     The Cassubian Civilization. London, 1935.

213. Ramult, Stefan. Słownik języka pomorskiego czyli
     kaszubskiego. Cracow, 1893.

214. Lorentz, Friedrich. Slovinzisches Wörterbuch.
     2 vols. St. Petersburg, 1908-1912.

215. Lehr-Spławiński,Tadeusz. Gramatyka połabska. Lwow,
     1929.

216. Trubetzkoy, N.S. Polabische Studien. Vienna, 1929.

217. Rost, Paul. Die Sprachreste der Draväno-Polaben.
     Leipzig, 1907.

Czech and Slovak

Modern Czech

218. Gebauer, Jan and Václav Ertl. Mluvnice česká pro
     školy střední a ústavy učitelské. 2 vols.
     Prague, 1930.

219. Trávníček, František. Mluvnice spisovné češtiny.
     2 vols. Prague, 1948-1949.

220. Vey, M. Morphologie du tchèque parlé. Paris, 1946.

221. Šmilauer, Vladimír. Novočeská skladba. Prague,
     1947.

222. Mathesius, Vilém. Čeština a obecný jazykozpyt.
     Prague, 1947.

223. Trávníček, František. Správná česká výslovnost.
     Brno, 1925.

224. -----. Úvod do české fonetiky. Prague, 1932.

225. Frinta, Antonín. Novočeská výslovnost. Prague,
     1909.

226. -----. A Czech Phonetic Reader. London, 1925.

227. Stanislav, Ján. Československá mluvnica. Prague, 1938.

228. Orlovský, J. and L. Arany. Gramatika jazyka slovenského. Bratislava, 1946.

229. Pauliny, Eugen. Štruktúra slovenského slovesa. Bratislava, 1943.

230. -----. Slovenské časovanie. Bratislava, 1949.

231. Letz, Belo. Kmeňoslovné úvahy. Turčiansky Sv. Martin, 1943.

History and Dialectology of Czech and Slovak

232. Hujer, Oldřich. Úvod do dějin jazyka českého. Prague, 1914, 1924 or 1946.

233. -----. "Vývoj jazyka československého," Českosloven ská vlastivěda, Vol. III (Prague, 1934), 1-83.

234. Havránek, Bohuslav. "Nářečí česká," Československá vlastivěda, Vol. III (Prague, 1934), 84-218.

235. Vážný, Václav. "Nářečí slovenská," Československá vlastivěda, Vol. III (Prague, 1934), 219-310.

236. Oberpfalcer, František. "Argot a slangy," Československá vlastivěda, Vol. III (Prague, 1934), 311-375.

237. Trávníček, František. Historická mluvnice československá. Prague, 1935.

238. Gebauer, Jan. Historická mluvnice jazyka českého . 4 vols. Prague, 1894-1929.

239. Skalička, Vladimír. Vývoj české deklinace. Prague, 1941.

240. Havránek, Bohuslav. "Vývoj spisovného jazyka českého, " Československá vlastivěda, Series II(Prague, 1936), 1-144.

241. Vážný, Václav. "Spisovný jazyk slovenský, " Československá vlastivěda, Series II (Prague, 1936), 145-215.

242. Pauliny, Eugen. Dejiny spisovnej slovenčiny. Bratislava, 1948.

243. Flajšhans, Václav. Nejstarší památky jazyka i písemnictví českého, Vol. I. Prague, 1903.

Dictionaries

244. Váša, Pavel and František Trávníček. Slovník jazyka českého. Prague, 1946.

245. Smetánka, Emil, Oldřich Hujer and Miloš Weingart. Příruční slovník jazyka českého. Prague: Česká akademie věd a umění, 1935 to date.

246. Gebauer, Jan. Slovník staročeský. 2 vols. Prague, 1903-1916.

247. Šimek, František. Slovníček staré češtiny. Prague, 1947.

248. Bartoš, F.M. Dialektologický slovník moravský. Prague, 1906.

249. Kálal, Miroslav. Slovenský slovník z literatúry aj nárečí. Banská Bystrica, 1923.

250. Holub, Josef. Stručný slovník etimologický jazyka česko-slovenského. Prague, 1933.

251. Osička, Antonín and Ivan Poldauf. Velký česko-
     anglický slovník. Prague, 1947.

252. -----. Velký anglicko-český slovník. Prague, 1948.

253. Konuš, J.J. Slovak-English and English-Slovak
     Dictionary. Pittsburgh, 1930, 1941.

Lusatian

254. Stieber, Zdzisław. Stosunki pokrewieństwa języków
     lużyckich. Cracow, 1934.

255. Schwela, Gotthold. Vergleichende Grammatik der
     ober-und nieder-sorbischen Sprache.
     Bautzen, 1926.

256. -----. Lehrbuch der niederwendischen Sprache.
     Vol. I, Heidelberg, 1906; Vol. II, Kottbus,
     1911.

257. Mucke, K.F. Historische und vergleichende Laut-
     und Formenlehre der niedersorbischen
     Sprache. Leipzig, 1891.

258. Mohelský, V. Mluvnice hornolužické srbštiny a
     slovník hornosrbsko-český. Olomouc, 1948.

259. Kral, Georg. Grammatik der wendischen Sprache in
     der Oberlausitz. Bautzen, 1935.

260. Щерба, Л.В. Восточнолужицкое наречие, Vol. I.
     St. Petersburg, 1915.

261. Wirth, Paul. Beiträge zum sorbischen (wendischen)
     Sprachatlas. 2 vols. Leipzig, 1933-1936.

262. Kral, Georg. Serbsko-němski słownik hornjołužiskeje
     rěče. Budyšin, 1931.

263. Мука, Эрнест. Словарь нижнелужицкого языка.
     3 vols. Prague, 1926-1928.

Introduction to South Slavic Languages

264. Snadfeld, Kristian. Linguistique balkanique.
     Paris, 1930.

266. Niederle, Lubor. Slovanské starožitnosti, Vol. I,
     Part II (Původ a počátky Slovanů jižních).
     Prague, 1906.

266. Skok, Petar. Dolazak slovena na Mediteran. Split,
     1934.

267. Vasmer, Max. Die Slaven in Griechenland.
     (Abhandlungen der preussischen Akademie
     der Wissenschaften, No. 12). Berlin, 1941.

Serbocroatian

Modern Serbocroatian

268. Meillet, Antoine and André Vaillant. Grammaire de
     la langue sertocroate. Paris, 1924.

269. Rešetar, Milan. Elementar-Grammatik der serbischen
     (croatischen) Sprache. Zagreb, 1916, 1922.
     Czech translation as: Mluvnice jazyka
     srbocharvátského. Prague, 1945.

270. Maretić, Tomislav. Gramatika i stilistika
     hrvatskoga ili srpskoga književnog jezika.
     Zagreb, 1899, 1931.

271. Ružić, R.H. The Aspects of the Verb in Serbo-
     Croatian (University of California
     Publications in Modern Philology, Vol.
     XXV, No. 2). Berkeley-Los Angeles, 1943.

272. Miletić, Branko. Les articulations serbo-croates.
(Bulletin de l'Académie des Lettres,
No. 1). Belgrade, 1935. Serb version as:
Изговор српско-хрватских гласова. (Српски
дијалектолошки зборник, Vol. V). Belgrade,
1933.

273. Belić, Aleksandar. "Srpskohrvatski jezik,"
"Čakavski dijalekt," "Kajkavski dijalekt,"
and "Štokavski dijalekt," Narodna
enciklopedija srpsko-hrvatsko-slovenačka.
4 vols. Zagreb, 1925-1929.

274. ------. Дијалекти источне и јужне Србије. (Српска
краљевска Академија наука. Српски
дијалектолошки зборник, Vol. I). Belgrade,
1905.

275. Даничић, Ђуро. Историја облика српскога или
хрватскога језика до свршетка XVII вијека.
Belgrade, 1874.

276. Кульбакин, С.М. Сербский язык. Kharkov, 1915.

277. Leskien, August. Grammatik der serbokroatischen
Sprache, Vol. I. Heidelberg, 1914.

278. Vaillant, André. La langue de Dominko Zlatarić,
poète ragusain de la fin du XVIe siècle.
2 vols. Paris, 1928-1931.

279. Rešetar, Milan. Der štokavische Dialekt. (Wiener
Akademie der Wissenschaften. Schriften
der Balkankommission). Vienna, 1907.

Development of Standard Serbocroatian

280. Poljanec, Franja. Istorija srpskohrvatskog
književnog jezika. Belgrade, 1931.

281. Murko, Matthias. "Die Bedeutung der Reformation
und Gegenreformation für das geistige
Leben der Südslaven," Slavia (Prague),
IV (1925-26), 499-522, 684-719; V (1926-
27), 65-99, 267-302, 500-534, 718-744.

282. Unbegaun, Boris. Les débuts de la langue littéraire chez les Serbes. Paris, 1935.

283. Новаковић, Стојан. Примери књижевности и језика старога и српско-словенскога. Belgrade, 1904.

284. Rešetar, Milan. Primorski lekcionari XV vijeka. (Jugoslavenska akademija znanosti i umjetnosti. Rad, Nos. 134, 136). Zagreb, 1898.

Dictionaries

285. Rječnik hrvatskoga ili srpskoga jezika. Zagreb: Jugoslavenska akademija, 1880 to date.

286. Караджић, Вук. Српски рјечник. Belgrade, 1898, 1935.

287. Даничић, Ђуро. Рјечник из књижевних старина српских. 3 vols. Belgrade, 1863-1864.

288. Bogadek, F.A. New English-Croatian and Croatian-English Dictionary. Pittsburgh, 1926.

289. Петровић, С.М. Енглеско-српски речник. Belgrade, 1936.

290. Djordjević, M.Ž. and R.M. Djurdjević. Srpsko-engleski rečnik. Hannover, 1948.

Slovenian

291. Ramovš, Franc. "Slovenački jezik," Narodna enciklopedija srpsko-hrvatsko-slovenačka (Zagreb, 1925-1929), IV, 192-208.

292. ------. Kratka zgodovina slovenskega jezika, Vol. I. Ljubljana, 1936.

293. Breznik, Anton. Slovenska slovnica za srednje šole. Mohorja, 1924 and Celje, 1934.

294. Bezlaj, F. Oris slovenskega knjižnega izgovora. Ljubljana, 1939.

295. Ramovš, Franc. Historična gramatika slovenskega jezika, Vols. II and VII. Ljubljana, 1924-1935.

296. ----. Karta slovenskih narečij v priročni izdaji. Ljubljana, 1935.

Dictionaries

297. Glonar, Joža. Slovar slovenskega jezika. Ljubljana, 1936.

298. Pleteršnik, M. Slovensko-nemški slovar. 2 vols. Ljubljana, 1894-1895.

299. Kotnik, F. Slovensko-angelški slovar. Ljubljana, 1945.

300. Kern, F.J. A Pronouncing English-Slovene Dictionary. Cleveland, 1944.

Macedonian

301. Кепески, К. Македонска граматика. Skopje, 1947.

302. Кочески, Б. Македонска литература и макесонскиот литературен јазик. Skopje, 1945.

303. Oblak, Vatroslav. Macedonische Studien (Sitzungsberichte der Wiener Akademie der Wissenschaften). Vienna, 1896.

304. Селищев, А.М. Очерки но македонской диалектологии. Kazan, 1918.

305. Małecki, Mieczysław. "Z zagadnień dialektologii macedońskiej," Focznik slawistyczny (Cracow), XVI (1938).

Bulgarian

Modern Bulgarian

306. Beaulieux, Léon. Grammaire de la langue bulgare.
Paris, 1933.

307. Младеновъ, Стефанъ. Граматика на българския
езикъ. Sofia, 1939.

308. Теодоровъ-Балачъ, Александъръ. Нова българска
граматика. Sofia, 1940.

309. Андрейчинъ, Л.Д. Основна българска граматика.
Sofia, 1944.

310. Andrejčin, L.D. Kategorie znaczeniowe konjugacji
bułgarskiej (Polska akademja umiejętności,
Prace komisji językowej, No. 26). Cracow,
1938.

311. Ekblom, Richard. "Zur bulgarischen Aussprache,"
Studier i modern sprakvetenskap, Vol. VI.
Upsala, 1917.

History and Dialectology of Fulgarian

312. Mladenov, Stefan. Geschichte der bulgarischen
Sprache (Grundriss der slavischen
Philologie und Kulturgeschichte, Vol. VI).
Berlin, 1929.

313. Младеновъ, Стефанъ. История на българскиятъ езикъ.
Sofia, 1935.

314. Цоневъ, Беньо. История на български езикъ. 3 vols.
Sofia, 1919-1937.

315. Miletič, Ljutomir. Das Ostbulgarische (Wiener
Akademie der Wissenschaften, Schriften
der Balkankommission). Vienna, 1903.

Dictionaries

316. Геровъ, Н. Рѣчникъ на български язикъ. 5 vols.
         Plovdiv, 1895-1904.

317. Младеновъ, Стефанъ, Александъръ Теодоровъ-Баланъ,
         et al. Български тълковенъ речникъ. Vol.
         I, Parts 1-10. Sofia, 1927-1948.

318. Младеновъ, Стефанъ. Етимологически и правописенъ
         речникъ на българския книжовенъ езикъ.
         Sofia, 1941.

319. Stefanov, Konstantin. Bulgarian-English Dictionary.
         Sofia, 1914.

320. Чакалов, Г. Англо-български речник. Sofia, 1948.

Bei Fragen zur Produktsicherheit wenden Sie sich bitte an:
If you have any questions regarding product safety,
please contact:

Walter de Gruyter GmbH
Genthiner Straße 13
10785 Berlin
productsafety@degruyterbrill.com